D1648943

Poetry Comprehension

Instruction · Practice · Assessment

Authors: Schyrlet Cameron and Suzanne Myers
Editor: Mary Dieterich
Proofreaders: April Albert and Margaret Brown

COPYRIGHT © 2016 Mark Twain Media, Inc.

ISBN 978-1-62223-594-0

Printing No. CD-404249

Mark Twain Media, Inc., Publishers
Distributed by Carson-Dellosa Publishing LLC

Visit us at www.carsondellosa.com

Table of Contents

Introduction

In recent years, there has been a renewed interest in the teaching of poetry. *Poetry Comprehension* provides students in grades six through eight the opportunity to explore this type of literature. Students can learn to appreciate the many forms of poetry that use figurative language, sound patterns, and word sounds to convey meaning in a powerful way. The book is designed to help students acquire the skills and practice the strategies needed to successfully perform on state assessments (online or print).

The book focuses on the English Language Arts Reading Standards for Literature. It is designed to help students acquire and apply the skills needed to analyze, interpret, and evaluate poetry. These skills will enable students to find the deeper meaning of a poem, which can lead to a new appreciation of this genre.

We selected a variety of poems with various levels of difficulty. Each poem was chosen to create interest and stimulate discussion. The text complexity of the poems require students to perform close reading.

This book is divided into three sections: Instructional Resources, Skill Builders, and Assessment Prep.

- **Instructional Resources** introduce the structures and elements of poetry. These handouts can be used as supplemental materials.

- **Skill Builders** contain fifteen mini-lessons that allow students to acquire or review skills needed to successfully analyze, interpret, and evaluate poetry. Each lesson focuses on a different skill, such as recognizing tone or identifying theme. Each lesson features a poem followed by a skill-building activity.

- **Assessment Poems and Preps** tests students' understanding of poetry. This section features fifteen poems followed by comprehension questions similar to the types of assessment items developed by the testing consortiums. There are two additional assessments. One is a comparison of two poems. The other is a comparison between reading a poem and listening to a video presentation of the poem.

Poetry Comprehension offers teachers a range of instructional options to meet the diverse learning styles and ability levels of middle-school students. The activities in this book are meant to supplement or enhance the regular classroom English Language Arts curriculum and can be used for independent practice and small-group or classroom instruction.

A matrix has been provided as a quick-reference guide for lesson planning. Its purpose is to identify skills addressed in the book.

Skill Chart

	Alliteration	Allusion	Hyperbole	Imagery	Metaphor	Onomatopoeia	Personification	Rhyme/Repetition	Rhythm	Simile	Structure	Symbolism	Theme	Tone/Mood	Word Meaning
Count That Day Lost	X								X		X		X		
Don't Give Up							X				X		X		
Escape at Bedtime		X									X		X		
The Flag Goes By				X				X			X	X	X	X	
The Flight of Youth	X							X					X		X
The Glory of the Day Was in Her Face					X					X	X			X	X
Hope											X			X	X
I Wandered Lonely as a Cloud			X								X		X		X
Love and Friendship	X									X	X		X	X	
Meeting at Night				X		X					X		X		
The Railway Train							X				X			X	X
The Sandpiper							X				X			X	X
Sea Fever				X			X						X		X
The Throstle							X				X			X	
The Tide Rises, the Tide Falls								X	X		X	X	X		X
Paired Poems															
A Poison Tree											X	X	X	X	X
Blight	X			X			X				X		X		X

Common Types of Poetry

Poetry is a way to communicate experiences, emotions, ideas, and thoughts using sound patterns, word sounds, and figurative language.

Ballad

narrative poem, usually a folk tale or legend, that is often sung

Limerick

humorous five-line poem that uses an AABBA rhyme scheme

Epic

long narrative poem that tells the story of a heroic or legendary figure

Lyric

short poem expressing the strong feelings or emotions of the speaker

Elegy

poem that expresses sorrow or mourning for someone who has died

Narrative

poem that tells a story

Free Verse

poem that does not use a fixed pattern of meter or rhyme

Ode

lyric poem celebrating a person, important event, or idea

Haiku

unrhymed poem consisting of 3 lines with each line having a 5-, 7-, and 5-syllable pattern

Sonnet

lyric poem consisting of 14 lines that expresses a thought or feeling

Ten Steps to Poetry Comprehension

1. **Preview the Poem**
    *   *Read the title and predict what the poem is about.*
    *   *Identify the poet.*

2. **Read the Poem**
    *   *Read the poem multiple times, both silently and aloud.*

3. **Create Mental Pictures**
    *   *As you read, visualize what is being described in the poem.*

4. **Examine Word Choice**
    *   *Determine the meaning of unfamiliar words by using decoding skills, context clues, or looking in a dictionary.*
    *   *Look for negative and positive word connotations to help determine tone and mood.*

5. **Paraphrase**
    *   *Restate the poem in order to clarify the content.*

6. **Analyze Structure and Organization**
    *   *Determine the overall organization of lines and stanzas.*
    *   *Notice special usage of punctuation and sentence breaks.*

7. **Identify Figurative Language**
    *   *Examine the poem for the poet's usage of figurative language (i.e.: similes, metaphors, imagery, personification, hyperbole, allusion).*

8. **Make Connections**
    *   *Link what you already know or have experienced to help understand allusions and symbolism.*

9. **Identify Sound Devices**
    *   *Examine the poem for the poet's usage of sound devices (i.e.: rhyme, rhythm, repetition, alliteration, onomatopoeia).*

10. **Synthesize**
    *   *Use your analysis to determine the theme or central idea of the poem.*

Glossary

Alliteration – the repeated use of the same consonant sound at the beginning of words that are near each other

Allusion – a brief reference to a biblical, historical, literary, or mythological person, place, thing, or idea

Hyperbole – a deliberate use of exaggeration for effect or to emphasize a point

Imagery – the use of words to create a vivid mental picture or physical sensation

Metaphor – a figure of speech that compares two unlike objects or ideas without using the words *like* or *as*

Mood – the emotions and feelings the poem arouses in the reader or audience

Onomatopoeia – a word that sounds like its meaning or mimics a sound

Personification – the giving of human characteristics to an animal, non-living object, or idea

Repetition – the repeated use of a word, phrase, line, or stanza in a poem

Rhyme – the pattern of correspondence of the end sounds of each line of a stanza or poem; also correspondence of sounds other than at the ends of lines

Rhythm – the sound pattern of a poem

Simile – a figure of speech used to compare two different things using the words *like* or *as*

Stanza – a series of lines grouped together and separated from other stanzas by a blank line

Structure – the overall organization of the lines

Symbolism – the use of a symbol (words, objects, or actions) to represent something other than itself

Theme – the main message or central idea of a poem

Tone – the poet's feelings (attitude) toward the subject of the poem

Poetry Websites

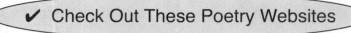

✔ Check Out These Poetry Websites

Academy of American Poets
http://www.poets.org/

All Poetry (Classics)
http://allpoetry.com/classics

The American Verse Project
http://quod.lib.umich.edu/a/amverse/

Bartleby.com
http://www.bartleby.com/verse/

Favorite Poem Project
http://www.favoritepoem.org/

Library of Congress (Poetry180/A Poem a Day for American High Schools)
http://www.loc.gov/poetry/180/p180-list.html

Middle School Poetry 180
https://middleschoolpoetry180.wordpress.com/the-poems/

Passions in Poetry
http://www.netpoets.com/poems/

PoemHunter.com
http://www.poemhunter.com/

The Poetry Archive
http://www.poetryarchive.org/

Poetry Out Loud
http://www.poetryoutloud.org/

Poetry Soup (Poems/Poem Search Engine)
http://www.poetrysoup.com/poems/

readwritethink (April is National Poetry Month!)
http://www.readwritethink.org/classroom-resources/calendar-activities/april-national-poetry-month-20478.html

09-02-2021

Name: _____ Date: _____

Alliteration

Alliteration is the repeated use of the same consonant sound at the beginning of words that are near each other.

> **Example:** *She sells sea-shells on the sea-shore.*

Poets use alliteration to direct attention to key words, create a rhythm, or reflect a tone.

> **Example:** *Good night, good night! Parting is such sweet sorrow,*
> (*Romeo and Juliet* by William Shakespeare)

Directions: Read the excerpt and follow the directions below.

Poem: "The Raven" [*The devil Bird*] by Edgar Allan Poe (excerpt)

Once upon a midnight dreary [*dull / depressing*], while I pondered, weak and weary [*showing tiredness*],
Over many a quaint [*old fashioned*] and curious volume of forgotten lore—
While I nodded, nearly napping, suddenly there came a tapping,
As of some one gently rapping, rapping at my chamber door.
"'Tis some visitor," I muttered, "tapping at my chamber door—
    Only this, and nothing more."

Ah, distinctly I remember it was in the bleak December,
And each separate dying ember wrought its ghost upon the floor.
Eagerly I wished the morrow;—vainly I had sought to borrow
From my books surcease of sorrow—sorrow for the lost Lenore—
For the rare and radiant maiden whom the angels name Lenore—
    Nameless *here* for evermore.

Public Domain

Explain the poet's purpose for using alliteration in the poem. Support your answer using examples of alliteration from the poem.

Write your answer in the box.

> The poet used alliterations to show how he feels for a loved one
> Dead. Some examples of alliteration is dreary, weary, napping,
> tapping, Morrow, borrow, Lenor, evermore

09-02-2021

Name: _____   Date: _____

Allusion

An **allusion** is a brief reference to a biblical, historical, literary, or mythological person, place, thing, or idea.

Hint: When a poet references something you are not familiar with, take time to research the reference in order to understand the meaning of the allusion.

Examples: *Chocolate is my <u>Achilles' heel</u>.* (mythological)
The neighbor's backyard is a <u>Garden of Eden</u>. (biblical)
She is such a <u>Scrooge</u>! (literary)

Directions: Read the poem and follow the directions.

Poem: "The World is Too Much with Us" by William Wordsworth

> The world is too much with us; late and soon,
> Getting and spending, we lay waste our powers;—
> Little we see in Nature that is ours.
> We have given our hearts away, a sordid boon!
> This Sea that bares her bosom to the moon,
> The winds that will be howling at all hours,
> And are up-gathered now like sleeping flowers;
> For this, for everything, we are out of tune;
> It moves us not. Great God! I'd rather be
> A Pagan, suckled in a creed outworn;
> So might I, standing on this pleasant lea,
> Have glimpses that would make me less forlorn;
> Have sight of Proteus rising from the sea,
> Or hear old Triton blow his wreathèd horn.

Public Domain

Identify **two** lines from the poem that contain allusions to mythological characters.

Write the lines in the box below.

Have sight of <u>proteus</u> rising from the sea

A pogan suckeled in a cred outworn

Name: _____   Date: _09 - 12 - 2021_

Hyperbole

Hyperbole is a figure of speech. It is a deliberate use of exaggeration for effect or to emphasize a point.

Examples: *The stray cat was* <u>*as skinny as a rail*</u> *when we rescued it.*
She could have <u>*knocked me over with a feather*</u>.
My computer is <u>*older than the hills*</u>.
I had <u>*a ton*</u> *of science homework.*

Directions: Read the stanza from the poem "Concord Hymn" and follow the directions below.

> **Poem:** "Concord Hymn" by Ralph Waldo Emerson
>
> By the rude bridge that arched the flood,
> Their flag to April's breeze unfurled,
> Here once the embattled farmers stood,
> And fired the shot heard round the world.
>
> Public Domain

1. Identify the hyperbole used in the stanza. Explain why it is an exaggeration.

Hyperbole: Fired the shot heard round the world.

Explanation: A Battle has started.

2. Locate **five** poems containing hyperbole. Complete the chart. Fill in the information under the correct column heading.

Title of Poem	Example of Hyperbole
To his coy mistress	Thine eyes on thy forehead gaze
The Iliad	as loudly as 9 or 10,000 men
a red red rose	Till a the seas gang dry, my dear
as I walked out one evening	and salmon sing in the street
I wandered lonely as a cloud	10,000 I saw at glance

Name: _____ Date: _09-12-2021_

Imagery

Imagery is the use of words to create a vivid mental picture or physical sensation. Poets use this figure of speech to appeal to a reader's senses (sight, sound, taste, smell, or even touch).

Example: *A host, of <u>golden</u> daffodils;* ("Daffodils" by William Wordsworth)

Hint: Imagery often uses other figures of speech such as simile, metaphor, personification, or onomatopoeia to help paint a mental picture.

Directions: Read the poem and follow the directions below.

Poem: "Lost" by Carl Sandburg

> Desolate and lone
> All night long on the lake
> Where fog trails and mist creeps,
> The whistle of a boat
> Calls and cries unendingly,
> Like some lost child
> In tears and trouble
> Hunting the harbor's breast
> And the harbor's eyes.
>
> Public Domain

Identify **four** examples of imagery from the poem. Use these examples to complete the chart. Fill in the information under the correct column heading.

Example of Imagery	Sense (sight, sound, taste, smell, touch)
where fog trails & mist creeps	sight
the whistle of the Boat	touch
In tears and trouble	sound
and the harbors eyes	sight

Name: _____ Date: _____

Metaphor

A **metaphor** is a figure of speech that compares two unlike objects or ideas without using the words *like* or *as*. A metaphor states that something **is** something else.

Example:

Metaphor	Two Things Being Compared	Meaning
Carl is a fountain of ideas.	*Carl and fountain*	*Carl has many ideas.*

Directions: Read the poem and follow the directions below.

Poem: "Wind and Window Flower" by Robert Frost

Lovers, forget your love,
  And list to the love of these,
She a window flower,
  And he a winter breeze.

When the frosty window veil
  Was melted down at noon,
And the cagèd yellow bird
  Hung over her in tune,

He marked her through the pane,
  He would not help but mark,
And only passed her by,
  To come again at dark.

He was a winter wind,
  Concerned with ice and snow,
Dead weeds and unmated birds,
  And little of love could know.

But he sighed upon the sill,
  He gave the sash a shake,
As witness all within
  Who lay that night awake.

Perchance he half prevailed
  To win her for the flight
From the firelit looking-glass
  And warm stove-window light.

But the flower leaned aside
  And thought of naught to say,
And morning found the breeze
  A hundred miles away.

Public Domain

Complete the chart by explaining the meaning of each metaphor.

Metaphor	Meaning
She a window flower,	Flower as in nice, pretty
And he a winter breeze.	Winter breeze as in cold, mean

11

Name: _____   Date: _____

Onomatopoeia

Onomatopoeia is a word that sounds like its meaning or mimics a sound. Poets use this sound device to create a mental image.

Examples: *beep, click,* and *ding*

Directions: Read the stanza from the poem "The Bells." Highlight the examples of onomatopoeia.

> **Poem:** "The Bells" by Edgar Allan Poe
>
> Hear the sledges with the bells—
> Silver bells!
> What a world of merriment their melody foretells!
> How they tinkle, tinkle, tinkle,
> In their icy air of night!
> While the stars, that over sprinkle
> All the heavens, seem to twinkle
> With a crystalline delight;
> Keeping time, time, time,
> In a sort of Runic rhyme,
> To the tintinnabulation that so musically wells
> From the bells, bells, bells, bells,
> Bells, bells, bells—
> From the jingling and the tinkling of the bells.
>
> Public Domain

Locate examples of onomatopoeia from **two** different poems. Use the examples to complete each graphic organizer. Fill in the correct information in each box.

Poem Title: *The bells* **Poet:** *Edgar Allan poe*	→	**Example of Onomatopoeia** *Bells*	→	**What does the sound mimic?** *Tinkle*
Poem Title: *meeting at night* **Poet:** *Robert Browning*	→	**Example of Onomatopoeia** *& in fiery ringlets from there sleep*	→	**What does the sound mimic?** *Ringlets*

Personification

    Personification is the giving of human characteristics to an animal, non-living object, or idea. Poets use this figure of speech to add interest, to create a mental image, or to help the reader understand a difficult concept.

        Examples: *Rick heard the last piece of <u>cake calling</u> his name.*
                The <u>headlights</u> of the oncoming car <u>winked</u> at us.
                <u>Time flies</u> when you are having fun.

Directions: Read the poem and follow the directions below.

> **Poem:** "Along the Road" by Robert Browning Hamilton
>
>   I walked a mile with Pleasure,
>   She chattered all the way;
>   But left me none the wiser,
>   For all she had to say.
>
>   I walked a mile with Sorrow
>   And ne'er a word said she;
>   But, oh, the things I learned from her
>   When Sorrow walked with me!
>
>   Public Domain

Choose **two** examples of personification from the poem. Use the examples to answer the questions.

Example #1 (line from the poem): *I walked a mile with pleasure.*

_____

What is being personified? *the word pleasure*

What human characteristic is being given? *pleasure and the person are walking*

Example #2 (line from the poem): *When Sorrow walked with me!*

_____

What is being personified? *the word sorrow*

What human characteristic is being given? *Sorrow is walking*

Name: _____   Date: *09-21-2021*

Rhyme/Repetition

Rhyme and **repetition** are sound devices poets use to make poems easier to memorize, emphasize a feeling, or clarify an idea.

- **Rhyme scheme** is the pattern of rhyme at the end of each line of a stanza or poem. To be a scheme, the pattern must be continued throughout the entire poem. Capital letters are used to mark the pattern of the rhyme.

Examples of Patterns

Pattern AABB

Twinkle, twinkle, little star, **A**
How I wonder what you are! **A**
Up above the world so high, **B**
Like a diamond in the sky. **B**

Pattern ABCB

Jack Sprat could eat no fat, **A**
His wife could eat no lean, **B**
And so, betwixt them both, **C**
They licked the platter clean. **B**

- **Repetition** is the repeated use of a word, phrase, line, or stanza in a poem.

Example of Repetition: Row, row, row, your boat
Gently down the stream
Merrily, merrily, merrily, merrily
Life is but a dream.

Directions: Read the poem. At the end of each line, mark the rhyme scheme. Then follow the directions below.

Poem: "The House on the Hill" by Edwin Arlin Robinson

They are all gone away,
    The House is shut and still,
There is nothing more to say.

Through broken walls and gray
    The winds blow bleak and shrill:
They are all gone away.

Nor is there one to-day
    To speak them good or ill:
There is nothing more to say.

Why is it then we stray
    Around that sunken sill?
They are all gone away,

And our poor fancy-play
    For them is wasted skill:
There is nothing more to say.

There is ruin and decay
    In the House on the Hill:
They are all gone away,
There is nothing more to say.

Public Domain

Explain the author's purpose for using repetition. Support your answer using textual evidence from the poem.

I think to write it more sad yet more intresting.

_____

_____

Rhythm

The **rhythm** or sound pattern of a poem is determined by the word choice of the poet. Rhythm can be created by emphasizing key words; repetition of certain words; or the stressed and unstressed parts of words in a line, stanza, or throughout the entire poem. Poets use rhythm to create an effect, mood, or picture in the mind of the reader.

Example: In this excerpt from the nursery rhyme, "Hickory Dickory Dock," both repetition and stressed and unstressed syllables are used to create the effect of a ticking clock.

> **Hick**ory **dick**ory **dock**,
> The **mouse** ran **up** the **clock**.
> The **clock** struck **one**,
> The **mouse** ran **down**,
> **Hick**ory **dick**ory **dock**.

Directions: Read the poem and follow the directions below.

Poem: "Windy Nights" by Robert Louis Stevenson

> Whenever the moon and the stars are set,
>   Whenever the wind is high,
> All night long in the dark and wet,
>   A man goes riding by.
> Late in the night when the fires are out,
> Why does he gallop and gallop about?
>
> Whenever the trees are crying aloud,
>   And ships are tossed at sea,
> By, on the highway, low and loud,
>   By at the gallop goes he.
> By at the gallop he goes, and then
> By he comes back at the gallop again.

Public Domain

Describe how the poet's repeated use of the word **gallop** contributes to the overall rhythm of the poem. Support your answer using textual evidence from the poem.

In the poem gallop means that he is constantly moving to places

Name: _____ Date: _____

Simile

A **simile** is a figure of speech used by poets to compare two different things using the words *like* or *as*. Poets use similes to describe ideas or feelings in a few words, make the poem more interesting, or add humor.

Examples:

Simile	Comparison	Alike
The road was <u>as smooth as glass</u>.	road and glass	smooth
Kim felt <u>like a duck out of water</u> at the party.	Kim and duck	awkward

Directions: Read the excerpt and follow the directions below.

> **Poem:** "A Red, Red Rose" by Robert Burns (excerpt)
>
> O my Luve's like a red, red rose,
>   That's newly sprung in June;
> O my Luve's like the melodie,
>   That's sweetly play'd in tune.
>
> As fair art thou, my bonnie lass,
>   So deep in luve am I;
> And I will luve thee still, my dear,
>   Till a' the seas gang dry.
>
> Till a' the seas gang dry, my dear,
>   And the rocks melt wi' the sun:
> I will luve thee still, my dear,
>   While the sands o' life shall run.
>
> Public Domain
>
> *gang* — gone
> *wi'* — with

Locate the **two** similes in stanza 1 of the poem. Complete the chart. Fill in the information for each simile under the correct column heading.

Simile (write lines from poem)	Two Things Being Compared	How are they alike?
Till a' the seas going dry, my dear	o my Luve's like the melodie	They are both talking about
And the Rocks melt wi' the sun	That's sweetly play'd in tune	They are both talking about Love.

Name: _____ Date: _____

Structure

The **structure** of a poem is the overall organization of the lines. Lines of a poem may vary in length. A poet may choose to place an entire sentence on a line or break the sentence into multiple lines.

Example:

Woodman, spare that tree!
Touch not a single bough!
In youth it shelter'd me,
And I'll protect it now;
'Twas my forefather's hand
That placed it near his cot;
There, Woodman, let it stand,
Thy axe shall harm it not!

("Woodman, Spare That Tree!" [excerpt] by George Pope Morris)

Stanzas are a series of lines grouped together and are separated from other stanzas by a blank line. Each stanza conveys an idea similar to a paragraph in an essay. A stanza may vary in the number of lines. Common types of stanzas are couplets (two rhyming lines), tercets (three lines that may or may not rhyme), and quatrains (four lines that may or may not rhyme). Many modern poems are free verse, which means they may not have any identifiable structure.

Directions: Read the poem and follow the directions below.

> **Poem:** "Who Has Seen the Wind" by Christina Rossetti
>
> Who has seen the wind?
> Neither I nor you:
> But when the leaves hang trembling,
> The wind is passing through.
>
> Who has seen the wind?
> Neither you nor I:
> But when the trees bow down their heads,
> The wind is passing by.
>
> Public Domain

1. Write the number of stanzas in the poem. _____ 1

2. Write the number of lines in each stanza. _____ 4

3. Underline a line in the poem that is a complete sentence.

4. Circle a sentence in the poem that is broken into multiple lines.

Name: _____   Date: _____

Symbolism

Symbolism is the use of a symbol (words, objects, or actions) to represent something other than itself. Poets use symbols to make a connection between the concept and something the reader is familiar with in life. The purpose of symbolism is to create a mood or strong feeling, to help the reader understand the poem, or to create a deeper meaning.

Examples:	**Symbol**	**Meaning**
	flag of the United States	*freedom*
	night	*death*

Directions: Read the poem and follow the directions below.

Poem: "The Eagle" by Alfred, Lord Tennyson

He clasps the crag with crooked hands;
Close to the sun in lonely lands,
Ring'd with the azure world, he stands.

The wrinkled sea beneath him crawls;
He watches from his mountain walls,
And like a thunderbolt he falls.

Public Domain

Complete the chart for the poem. An example has been provided.

Symbol	What does the word or phrase represent?
1. eagle	power; authority; superiority
2. crooked hands	mistaken, weak
3. lonely lands	lonely, lose some,
4. mountain walls	Strong
5. thunderbolt	Threatining

Brish

Name: _____   Date: 10-15-2024

Theme

    Theme is the main message or central idea of a poem. It is revealed in the poet's choice of words. Close reading must be used to determine the theme. Some common themes are birth, death, freedom, survival, friendship, and patriotism.

Directions: Read the poem and follow the directions below.

Poem: "The Rainy Day" by Henry Wadsworth Longfellow

    The day is cold, and dark, and dreary;
    It rains, and the wind is never weary;
    The vine still clings to the moldering wall,
    But at every gust the dead leaves fall,
        And the day is dark and dreary!

    My life is cold, and dark, and dreary;
    It rains, and the wind is never weary;
    My thoughts still cling to the moldering Past,
    But the hopes of youth fall thick in the blast,
        And the days are dark and dreary.

    Be still, sad heart! And cease repining;
    Behind the clouds is the sun still shining;
    Thy fate is the common fate of all,
    Into each life some rain must fall,
        Some days must be dark and dreary.

                    Public Domain

Explain the theme of the poem. Use details from the poem to support your answer.

Write your answer in the box.

> The theme is how his life is dark & weary. He keeps on thinking about the past & has a depressing past which he's comparing with the weather

Name: _____   Date: ___10-19-2021___

Tone and Mood

Often a word used to describe tone can also be used to describe mood. Poets create tone and mood by word choice and the use of figurative language. **Tone** is how a poet feels (attitude) toward the subject of the poem. **Mood** (atmosphere) is the emotions and feelings the poem arouses in the reader. Authors choose words with positive or negative connotations in order to influence the way a reader thinks or feels.

Words That Describe Tone (attitude)		Words That Describe Mood (atmosphere)	
Positive Connotation	Negative Connotation	Positive Connotation	Negative Connotation
calm	*annoyed*	*peaceful*	*dreary*
cheerful	*impatient*	*joyous*	*scared*

Directions: Read the poem and follow the directions below.

Poem: "The Pasture" by Robert Frost

I'm going out to clean the pasture spring;
I'll only stop to rake the leaves away
(And wait to watch the water clear, I may):
I sha'n't be gone long.—You come too.

I'm going out to fetch the little calf
That's standing by the mother. It's so young,
It totters when she licks it with her tongue.
I sha'n't be gone long.—You come too.

Public Domain

Complete the charts for tone and mood. Fill in the information under the correct column headings.

What is the tone of the poem?	List words that help identify the tone.	Do <u>most</u> of the words have a positive or negative connotation?
calm	I'm going out to fetch the little calf	Positive
What is the mood of the poem?	**List words that help identify the mood.**	**Do <u>most</u> of the words have a positive or negative connotation?**
peaceful	It totters when she licks it with her tongue	Positive.

Name: _____   Date: _____

Word Meaning

When reading a poem, you may encounter unfamiliar words. Figure out the meaning of these words by using decoding skills and context clues.

Hint: Adding a prefix or suffix to a root or base word makes a new word with a new meaning.

Directions: Read the excerpt and follow the directions below.

> **Poem:** "A Song" by James Whitcomb Riley (excerpt)
>
> There is ever a song somewhere, my dear,
>   There is ever a something sings alway:
> There's the song of the lark when the skies are clear,
>   And the song of the thrush when the skies are gray.
> The sunshine showers across the grain,
>   And the bluebird <u>trills</u> in the orchard tree;
> And in and out, when the eaves drip rain,
>   The swallows are twittering ceaselessly.
>   Public Domain

Complete the graphic organizer for the word **trills** as it is used in the poem.

What do you think this word means?	What words or phrases provide context clues for the meaning of the word?
Write the dictionary meaning for the word.	**Write the best synonym for the word.**

trills

Poet: George Eliot (1819–1880)
Birthplace: England
Interesting Fact: George Eliot was the pen name for Mary Ann Evans. Some of her most famous novels are *Adam Bede, Middlemarch,* and *Silas Marner.*

Count That Day Lost

If you sit down at set of sun
And count the acts that you have done,
And, counting, find
One self-denying deed, one word
That eased the heart of him who heard,
One glance most kind
That fell like sunshine where it went—
Then you may count that day well spent.

But if, through all the livelong day,
You've cheered no heart, by yea or nay—
If, through it all
You've nothing done that you can trace
That brought the sunshine to one face—
No act most small
That helped some soul and nothing cost—
Then count that day as worse than lost.

—George Eliot

Assessment Questions: "Count That Day Lost"

1. Which statement **best** reflects the theme of the poem?
   - ○ A. Do not miss the opportunity to help others.
   - ○ B. Perform good deeds every day.
   - ○ C. Good behavior brings happiness to others.
   - ● D. A person is responsible for their own actions.

2. Why does the speaker **most likely** repeat the word *you* in stanza 1?
   - ● A. to encourage readers to be responsible for their own actions
   - ○ B. to demonstrate the importance of helping others
   - ○ C. to emphasize the consequences of poor behavior
   - ○ D. to stress the identity of the intended audience

3. Alliteration is the repetition of a consonant sound at the beginning of a series of words. Which line from the poem contains alliteration?
   - ● A. *If you sit down at set of sun*
   - ○ B. *And, counting, find*
   - ○ C. *One glance most kind*
   - ○ D. *No act most small*

4. Based upon the poem, what generalization can the reader make about the speaker?
   - ● A. The speaker believes in the importance of doing good deeds.
   - ○ B. The speaker enjoys being around other people.
   - ○ C. The speaker thinks some acts of kindness are too small to perform.
   - ○ D. The speaker feels everyone should rely on themselves.

5. Explain how the last stanza contributes to the theme of the poem. Use textual evidence from the poem to support your answer.

   Write your answer in the box.

Poet: Phoebe Cary (1824–1871)
Birthplace: Ohio
Interesting Fact: Cary was an activist for women's rights.

Don't Give Up

If you've tried and have not won,
    Never stop for crying;
All that's great and good is done
    Just by patient trying.

Though young birds, in flying, fall,
    Still their wings grow stronger;
And the next time they can keep
    Up a little longer.

Though the sturdy oak has known
    Many a blast that bowed her,
She has risen again, and grown
    Loftier and prouder.

If by easy work you beat,
    Who the more will prize you?
Gaining victory from defeat,—
    That's the test that tries you!

—Phoebe Cary

10-28-21

Name: _____ Date: _____

Assessment Questions: "Don't Give Up"

1. How many lines are in each stanza?
   - ○ A. 3
   - ◉ B. 4
   - ○ C. 12
   - ○ D. 16

2. Which stanza has a different rhyme scheme than the other stanzas?
   - ○ A. stanza 1
   - ○ B. stanza 2
   - ○ C. stanza 3
   - ◉ D. stanza 4

3. Based upon the poem, what generalization can the reader make about the speaker's personality?
   - ○ A. The speaker is sentimental.
   - ○ B. The speaker is pessimistic.
   - ◉ C. The speaker is optimistic.
   - ○ D. The speaker is judgmental.

4. **Part A**

   Which word **best** describes the theme of the poem?
   - ◉ A. courage
   - ○ B. defeat
   - ○ C. perseverance
   - ○ D. victory

   Part B

   Which stanza from the poem is the **most** helpful in determining the theme?
   - ◉ A. stanza 1
   - ○ B. stanza 2
   - ○ C. stanza 3
   - ○ D. stanza 4

5. Explain the meaning of the last stanza of the poem.

   Write your answer in the box.

   > If you work hard to your defeat you still have victory.

Poet: Robert Louis Stevenson (1850–1894)
Birthplace: Scotland
Interesting Fact: Stevenson's most famous works are *Treasure Island* and *The Strange Case of Dr. Jekyll and Mr. Hyde.*

Escape at Bedtime

The lights from the parlour and kitchen shone out
    Through the blinds and the windows and bars;
And high overhead and all moving about,
    There were thousands of millions of stars.
There ne'er were such thousands of leaves on a tree,
    Nor of people in church or the Park,
As the crowds of the stars looked down upon me,
    And that glittered and winked in the dark.

The Dog, and the Plough, and the Hunter, and all,
    And the star of the sailor, and Mars,
These shone in the sky, and the pail by the wall
    Would be half full of water and stars.
They saw me at last, and they chased me with cries,
    And they soon had me packed into bed;
But the glory kept shining and bright in my eyes,
    And the stars going round in my head.

—Robert Louis Stevenson

10-28-21

Name: _____ Date: _____

Assessment Questions: "Escape at Bedtime"

1. What does stanza 2 reveal about the speaker?
   - ⊙ A. The speaker was fascinated with the multitude of stars.
   - ○ B. The speaker spent too much time looking at stars.
   - ○ C. The speaker tried to catch the stars in a pail of water.
   - ○ D. The speaker wanted to learn more about constellations.

2. An allusion is a brief reference to a biblical, historical, literary, or mythological person, place, thing, or idea. Which line from the poem contains allusion?
   - ○ A. *There were thousands of millions of stars.*
   - ⊙ B. *And that glittered and winked in the dark.*
   - ○ C. *The Dog, and the Plough, and the Hunter, and all,*
   - ○ D. *But the glory kept shining and bright in my eyes,*

3. **Part A**
   Which word **best** describes the theme of the poem?
   - ○ A. bedtime
   - ○ B. constellations
   - ⊙ C. stargazing
   - ○ D. trees

   Part B
   Which lines from the poem **best** support your answer?
   - ⊙ A. *And high overhead and all moving about,/There were thousands of millions of stars.*
   - ○ B. *As the crowds of the stars looked down upon me,/And that glittered and winked in the dark.*
   - ○ C. *These shone in the sky, and the pail by the wall,/Would be half full of water and stars.*
   - ○ D. *But the glory kept shining and bright in my eyes,/And the stars going round in my head.*

4. Which **two** lines from the poem **most likely** suggest that the speaker is a child?
   - ○ A. *The lights from the parlour and kitchen shone out*
   - ○ B. *And high overhead and all moving about,*
   - ○ C. *As the crowds of the stars looked down upon me,*
   - ○ D. *They saw me at last, and they chased me with cries,*
   - ○ E. *And they soon had me packed into bed;*
   - ⊙ F. *But the glory kept shining and bright in my eyes,*

5. Which line from the poem **best** reveals the setting of stanza 1?
   - ○ A. *The lights from the parlour and the kitchen shone out*
   - ○ B. *There ne'er were such thousands of leaves on a tree,*
   - ○ C. *Nor of people in church or the Park,*
   - ⊙ D. *As the crowds of the stars looked down upon me,*

Poet: Henry Holcomb Bennett (1863–1924)
Birthplace: Ohio
Interesting Fact: Bennett's poems were mainly published in newspapers or magazines.

The Flag Goes By

Hats off!
Along the street there comes
A blare of bugles, a ruffle of drums,
A flash of color beneath the sky:
Hats off!
The flag is passing by!

Blue and crimson and white it shines,
Over the steel-tipped, ordered lines.
Hats off!
The colors before us fly;
But more than the flag is passing by.

Sea-fights and land-fights, grim and great,
Fought to make and to save the State:
Weary marches and sinking ships;
Cheers of victory on dying lips;

Days of plenty and years of peace;
March of a strong land's swift increase;
Equal justice, right and law,
Stately honor and reverend awe;

Sign of a nation, great and strong
To ward her people from foreign wrong:
Pride and glory and honor,—all
Live in the colors to stand or fall.

Hats off!
Along the street there comes
A blare of bugles, a ruffle of drums;
And loyal hearts are beating high:
Hats off!
The flag is passing by!

—Henry Holcomb Bennett

Name: _____ Date: _____

Assessment Questions: "The Flag Goes By"

1. **Part A**
   Based upon the poem, what does a flag represent or symbolize?
   - ● A. freedom
   - ○ B. nation
   - ○ C. victory
   - ○ D. war

   Part B
   Which stanza **best** supports the answer in Part A?
   - ● A. stanza 1
   - ○ B. stanza 2
   - ○ C. stanza 4
   - ○ D stanza 5

2. Read the two lines repeated in the poem and answer the question.

   > Hats off!
   > The flag is passing by!

   What is **most likely** the significance of the poet's use of repetition?
   - ○ A. to inform readers about flag etiquette
   - ○ B. to recognize the significance of having flags in a parade
   - ● C. to emphasize the showing of respect for the flag
   - ○ D. to celebrate the tradition of flags leading a parade

3. Which word **best** describes the mood of the poem?
   - ○ A. confused
   - ○ B. excited
   - ○ C. powerful
   - ● D. proud

4. Which line from the poem is an example of imagery?
   - ● A. *A blare of bugles, a ruffle of drums.*
   - ○ B. *The colors before us fly;*
   - ○ C. *Equal justice, right and law,*
   - ○ D. *Pride and glory and honor,—all*

5. Which word **best** reflects the **key** theme of the poem?
   - ● A. freedom
   - ○ B. loyalty
   - ○ C. patriotism
   - ○ D. respect

Poet: Richard Henry Stoddard (1825–1903)
Birthplace: Massachusetts
Interesting Fact: Stoddard spent most of his life living in New York City.

The Flight of Youth

There are gains for all our losses,
  There are balms for all our pain:
But when youth, the dream, departs,
It takes something from our hearts,
  And it never comes again.

We are stronger, and are better,
  Under manhood's sterner reign:
Still we feel that something sweet
Followed youth, with flying feet,
  And will never come again.

Something beautiful is vanished,
  And we sigh for it in vain:
We behold it everywhere,
On the earth; and in the air,
  But it never comes again.

—Richard Henry Stoddard

Name: _____   Date: _____

Assessment Questions: "The Flight of Youth"

1. Read the lines from stanza 2 of the poem and answer the question.

   > We are stronger, and are better,
   > Under manhood's <u>sterner</u> reign:

   Which word is the **best** synonym for *sterner* as it is used in the stanza?
   - ○ A. firmer
   - ○ B. harsher
   - ○ C. sober
   - ○ D. tougher

2. Why does the speaker **most likely** repeat the phrase "never comes again"?
   - ○ A. to encourage the reader to never stop dreaming
   - ○ B. to help the reader memorize the poem
   - ○ C. to emphasize to the reader that when youth fades it doesn't return
   - ○ D. to inform the reader that growing old is better than remaining young

3. **Part A**
   Which phrase **best** describes the theme of the poem?
   - ○ A. loss of childhood
   - ○ B. life is full of losses
   - ○ C. adulthood is better than childhood
   - ○ D. dreams are only for the young

   Part B
   Which line from the poem is the **most** helpful in understanding the theme?
   - ○ A. *There are balms for all our pain;*
   - ○ B. *But when youth, the dream, departs,*
   - ○ C. *Followed youth with flying feet,*
   - ○ D. *Something beautiful is vanished*

4. Alliteration is the repetition of a consonant sound at the beginning of a series of words. Which **two** lines from the poem contain alliteration?
   - ○ A. *There are balms for all our pain;*
   - ○ B. *But when youth, the dream, departs,*
   - ○ C. *Under manhood's sterner reign;*
   - ○ D. *Followed youth with flying feet,*
   - ○ E. *And we sigh for it in vain;*
   - ○ F. *On the earth and in the air,*

5. What is **most likely** the poet's purpose for writing the poem?
   - ○ A. to inform readers that every person will grow older
   - ○ B. to share with readers feelings of sadness over lost youth
   - ○ C. to persuade readers to keep on dreaming
   - ○ D. to entertain readers with a poem about childhood

Poet: James Weldon Johnson (1871–1938)
Birthplace: Florida
Interesting Fact: Johnson was a civil rights leader in the early twentieth century.

The Glory of the Day Was in Her Face

The glory of the day was in her face,
The beauty of the night was in her eyes.
And over all her loveliness, the grace
Of Morning blushing in the early skies.

And in her voice, the calling of the dove;
Like music of a sweet, melodious part.
And in her smile, the breaking light of love;
And all the gentle virtues in her heart.

And now the glorious day, the beauteous night,
The birds that signal to their mates at dawn,
To my dull ears, to my tear-blinded sight
Are one with all the dead, since she is gone.

—James Weldon Johnson

Name: _____ Date: _____

Assessment Questions:
"The Glory of the Day Was in Her Face"

1. Read stanza 2 from the poem and answer the question.

    > *And in her voice, the calling of the dove;*
    > *Like music of a sweet, melodious part.*
    > *And in her smile, the breaking light of love;*
    > *And all the gentle virtues in her heart.*

    Which word is the **best** synonym for *virtues* as it is used in the stanza?
    - ○ A. assets
    - ● C. morals
    - ○ B. features
    - ○ D. qualities

2. Read these lines from the poem and answer the question.

    > *And in her voice, the calling of the dove;*
    > *Like music of a sweet, melodious part.*

    What does the comparison **most closely** suggest about the female?
    - ○ A. her voice sounds like the cooing of a dove
    - ○ B. her voice sounds pleasant to the ear
    - ○ C. her voice attracts unwanted attention
    - ○ D. her voice attracts the attention of doves

3. What feeling does the speaker express in the last stanza of the poem?
    - ○ A. guilt, because he never told her how he felt before she left
    - ○ B. hope, that she might return to him one day
    - ○ C. rejection, because she left him all alone
    - ○ D. sorrow, because she is no longer in his presence

4. To what does the poet compare "the beauty of the night"?
    - ○ A. her eyes
    - ○ C. her grace
    - ○ B. her face
    - ○ D. her voice

5. Explain how the tone of the poem changes in stanza 3. Use textual evidence from the poem to support your answer.

    Write your answer in the box.

    > Tone is the tone of regret. This sentence says it all ore one with all
    > the dead, since she is gone.

Poet: Emily Brontë (1818–1848)
Birthplace: England
Interesting Fact: Brontë is best known for her novel *Wuthering Heights*.

Hope

Hope Was but a timid friend;
She sat without the grated den,
Watching how my fate would tend,
Even as selfish-hearted men.

She was cruel in her fear;
Through the bars one dreary day,
I looked out to see her there,
And she turned her face away!

Like a false guard, false watch keeping,
Still, in strife, she whispered peace;
She would sing while I was weeping;
If I listened, she would cease.

False she was, and unrelenting;
When my last joys strewed the ground,
Even Sorrow saw, repenting,
Those sad relics scattered round;

Hope, whose whisper would have given
Balm to all my frenzied pain,
Stretched her wings, and soared to heaven,
Went, and ne'er returned again!

—Emily Brontë

Assessment Questions: "Hope"

1. Read the line from the poem and answer the question.

    > *False she was, and <u>unrelenting</u>;*

    What is the meaning of the prefix *-un* as it is used in the word *unrelenting*?
    - Ⓐ A. against
    - ◯ B. before
    - ◯ C. not
    - ◯ D. without

2. Read the line from the poem and answer the question.

    > *If I listened, she would <u>cease</u>.*

    Which word is the **best** synonym for *cease* as it is used in the line?
    - ◯ A. conclude
    - ◯ B. expire
    - ◯ C. finish
    - Ⓓ D. stop

3. Read the dictionary entry and answer the question.

    > **guard** \'gärd\ 1. a safety device 2. one who is assigned to protect 3. a position on a basketball team 4. a defensive attitude

    Which is the definition for the word *guard* as it is used in stanza 3?
    - ◯ A. definition 1
    - ◯ B. definition 2
    - ◯ C. definition 3
    - Ⓓ D. definition 4

4. Explain how the tone of the poem changes in stanza 5. Use evidence from the poem to support your answer.

    Write your answer in the box.

    > The tone went depressing on this sentence "he went, and ne'er returned again."

Poet: William Wordsworth (1770–1850)
Birthplace: England
Interesting Fact: Wordsworth was appointed Poet Laureate of England in 1843 and held this office until his death.

I Wandered Lonely as a Cloud
(aka Daffodils)

I wandered lonely as a cloud
That floats on high o'er vales and hills,
When all at once I saw a crowd,
A host, of golden daffodils;
Beside the lake, beneath the trees,
Fluttering and dancing in the breeze.

Continuous as the stars that shine
And twinkle on the milky way,
They stretched in never-ending line
Along the margin of a bay:
Ten thousand saw I at a glance,
Tossing their heads in sprightly dance.

The waves beside them danced; but they
Out-did the sparkling waves in glee:
A poet could not but be gay,
In such a jocund company:
I gazed—and gazed—but little thought
What wealth the show to me had brought:

For oft, when on my couch I lie
In vacant or in pensive mood,
They flash upon that inward eye
Which is the bliss of solitude;
And then my heart with pleasure fills,
And dances with the daffodils.

—William Wordsworth

Name: _____ Date: _____

Assessment Questions:
"I Wandered Lonely as a Cloud" (aka "Daffodils")

1. Read the dictionary entry and answer the question.

   > **host** \hōst\ n 1. an army assembled for battle 2. one who extends hospitality to another person 3. multitude or huge number 4. emcee of a television show

   Which is the definition for the word *host* as it is used in stanza 1?
   - ○ A. definition 1
   - ○ B. definition 2
   - ⊘ C. definition 3
   - ○ D. definition 4

2. Read the line from the poem and answer the question.

   > *Ten thousand saw I at a glance,*

   What does the hyperbole in the line above **most likely** reveal about the speaker?
   - ⊘ A. The speaker was in awe of the vast number of daffodils.
   - ○ B. The speaker was unable to count the number of daffodils.
   - ○ C. The speaker did not enjoy looking at daffodils.
   - ○ D. The speaker's favorite flower is the daffodil.

3. Which sentence **best** summarizes the meaning of the poem?
   - ○ A. Daffodils are beautiful flowers that bloom in the spring.
   - ○ B. Joy can be found in taking long walks along the beach.
   - ⊘ C. Taking long walks is a healthy activity people enjoy.
   - ○ D. Even the most insignificant event can create a lasting memory.

4. Read the two lines from stanza 3 of the poem and answer the question.

   > *I gazed—and gazed—but little thought*
   > *What wealth the show to me had brought:*

   Explain how the two lines from stanza 3 contribute to the meaning of stanza 4. Support your answer using textual evidence from the poem.

   Write your answer in the box.

   > when he's on the couch he remembers daffodils

Poet: Emily Brontë (1818–1848)
Birthplace: England
Interesting Fact: Brontë is best known for her novel *Wuthering Heights*.

Love and Friendship

Love is like the wild rose-briar,
Friendship like the holly-tree—
The holly is dark when the rose-briar blooms
But which will bloom most constantly?

The wild rose-briar is sweet in spring,
Its summer blossoms scent the air;
Yet wait till winter comes again
And who will call the wild-briar fair?

Then, scorn the silly rose-wreath now
And deck thee with the holly's sheen,
That, when December blights thy brow
He still may leave thy garland green.

—Emily Brontë

briar – a plant with a thorny or prickly stem

Name: _____   Date: _____

Assessment Questions: "Love and Friendship"

1. Which word **best** describes the tone of stanzas 1 and 2?
   - ○ A. accusing
   - ~~○ B. loving~~
   - ○ C. questioning ✓
   - ○ D. threatening

2. Alliteration is the repetition of a consonant sound at the beginning of a series of words. Which line from the poem contains alliteration?
   - ● A. *Friendship like the holly-tree—*
   - ○ B. *And who will call the wild-briar fair?*
   - ○ C. *And deck thee with the holly's sheen,*
   - ○ D. *He still may leave thy garland green.*

3. Which line from the poem **most likely** suggests the speaker prefers friendship over love?
   - ○ A. *Love is like the wild rose-brier,*
   - ○ B. *Friendship like the holly-tree—*
   - ○ C. *But which will bloom most constantly?*
   - ✓ ● D. *Then, scorn the silly rose-wreath now*

4. Explain why the poet compares love to a wild-rose briar. Support your answer using textual evidence from the poem.

   Write your answer in the box.

   > Because love like the rose blooms

5. Explain how stanza 3 contributes to the meaning of the poem. Support your answer using textual evidence from the poem.

   Write your answer in the box.

   > Stanza 3 accepts that their friendship is confusing.

Poet: Robert Browning (1812–1889)
Birthplace: England
Interesting Fact: Browning's courtship of the famous poet Elizabeth Barrett was conducted in secret.

Meeting at Night

The gray sea and the long black land;
And the yellow half-moon large and low:
And the startled little waves that leap
In fiery ringlets from their sleep,
As I gain the cove with pushing prow,
And quench its speed i' the slushy sand.

Then a mile of warm sea-scented beach;
Three fields to cross till a farm appears;
A tap at the pane, the quick sharp scratch
And blue spurt of a lighted match,
And a voice less loud, through its joys and fears,
Than the two hearts beating each to each!

—Robert Browning

Name: _____   Date: _____

Assessment Questions: "Meeting at Night"

1. **Part A**

   Which word **best** reflects the key theme of the poem?
   - ○ A. exploration
   - ○ B. love
   - ○ C. nighttime
   - ○ D. sailing

   Part B

   Which line from the poem is the **most** helpful in understanding the **key** theme?
   - ○ A. *And the yellow half-moon large and low:*
   - ○ B. *As I gain the cove with pushing prow,*
   - ○ C. *And a voice less loud, thro' its joys and fears,*
   - ○ D. *Than the two hearts beating each to each!*

2. Which phrase from the poem is **not** an example of imagery?
   - ○ A. *gray sea*
   - ○ B. *yellow half-moon*
   - ○ C. *quench its speed*
   - ○ D. *slushy sand*

3. Which line from the poem **best** indicates that the meeting at night is secretive?
   - ○ A. *And the yellow half-moon large and low:*
   - ○ B. *And quench its speed i' the slushy sand.*
   - ○ C. *Three fields to cross till a farm appears;*
   - ○ D. *A tap at the pane, the quick sharp scratch*

4. Why does the poet **most likely** use the words *tap*, *scratch*, and *spur*?
   - ○ A. to create a mental image
   - ○ B. to identify sounds heard by the speaker
   - ○ C. to add interest to the poem
   - ○ D. to reveal the secretive nature of the meeting

5. Explain how the last stanza contributes to the meaning of the poem. Support your answer using textual evidence from the poem.

   Write your answer in the box.

   ┌───┐
   │   │
   │   │
   │   │
   │   │
   │   │
   │   │
   └───┘

Poet: Emily Dickinson (1830–1886)
Birthplace: Massachusetts
Interesting Fact: Dickinson lived the last portion of her life as a recluse.

The Railway Train

I like to see it lap the miles,
And lick the valleys up,
And stop to feed itself at tanks;
And then, prodigious, step

Around a pile of mountains,
And, supercilious peer
In shanties by the sides of roads;
And there a quarry pare

To fit its sides, and crawl between,
Complaining all the while
In horrid, hooting stanza;
Then chase itself down hill

And neigh like Boanerges;
Then, punctual as a star,
Stop—docile and omnipotent—
At its own stable door.

—Emily Dickinson

supercilious – arrogant
pare – shave away; trim
Boanerges – "sons of thunder," [allusion to a Biblical verse (Mark 3:17)]
omnipotent – possessing unlimited power; supreme

Name: _____   Date: _____

Assessment Questions: "The Railway Train"

1. Which statement **best** explains the purpose of the title?
   ○ A. It helps the reader determine the tone of the poem.
   ○ B. It emphasizes the importance of traveling by train.
   ○ C. It reveals the subject of the poem.
   ○ D. It creates a mental image in the reader's mind.

2. Which word **best** describes the mood of the poem?
   ○ A. confused
   ○ B. fascinated
   ○ C. interested
   ○ D. puzzled

3. Explain the poet's use of words with negative connotations. Support your answer using textual evidence from the poem.

   Write your answer in the box.

   [   ]

4. Identify **five** examples of the poet's use of personification in the poem. Explain how the poet's use of personification contributes to the imagery of the poem.

   Write your answer in the box.

   [   ]

Poet: Celia Thaxter (1835–1894)
Birthplace: New Hampshire
Interesting Fact: Thaxter's childhood was spent living on an island.

The Sandpiper

Across the lonely beach we flit,
One little sandpiper and I,
And fast I gather, bit by bit,
The scattered driftwood, bleached and dry.
The wild waves reach their hands for it,
The wild wind raves, the tide runs high,
As up and down the beach we flit,—
One little sandpiper and I.

Above our heads the sullen clouds
Scud, black and swift, across the sky;
Like silent ghosts in misty shrouds
Stand out the white lighthouses high.
Almost as far as eye can reach
I see the close-reefed vessels fly,
As fast we flit along the beach,—
One little sandpiper and I.

I watch him as he skims along,
Uttering his sweet and mournful cry;
He starts not at my fitful song,
Nor flash of fluttering drapery.
He has no thought of any wrong,
He scans me with a fearless eye:
Staunch friends are we, well tried and strong,
The little sandpiper and I.

Comrade, where wilt thou be to-night,
When the loosed storm breaks furiously?
My driftwood fire will burn so bright!
To what warm shelter canst thou fly?
I do not fear for thee, though wroth
The tempest rushes through the sky:
For are we not God's children both,
Thou, little sandpiper, and I?

—Celia Thaxter

Name: _____ Date: _____

Assessment Questions: "The Sandpiper"

1. Which line is the **most** helpful in understanding the setting of this poem?
    - ○ A. *The scattered driftwood, bleached and dry.*
    - ○ B. *As up and down the beach we flit, —*
    - ○ C. *One little sandpiper and I.*
    - ○ D. *My driftwood fire will burn so bright!*

2. Which word **best** describes the mood of the last stanza of the poem?
    - ○ A. confident
    - ○ B. doubtful
    - ○ C. fearful
    - ○ D. worried

3. Read the dictionary entry and answer the question.

    > **comrade** \'käm-rad\ n 1. fellow soldier 2. close friend 3. one who shares the same interests and activities 4. member of the Communist party

    Which is the **best** definition for the word comrade as it is used in stanza 4?
    - ○ A. definition 1
    - ○ B. definition 2
    - ○ C. definition 3
    - ○ D. definition 4

4. Which rhyme pattern is used in stanza 1 of the poem?
    - ○ A. AABBCCDD
    - ○ B. ABABABAB
    - ○ C. ABCABCAB
    - ○ D. AABBAABB

5. Explain why the poet **most likely** repeats the phrase "little sandpiper and I" in each stanza of the poem.

    Write your answer in the box.

Poet: John Masefield (1878–1967)
Birthplace: England
Interesting Fact: In addition to poetry, Masefield also wrote children's novels.

Sea Fever

I must down to the seas again, to the lonely sea and the sky,
And all I ask is a tall ship and a star to steer her by;
And the wheel's kick and the wind's song and the white sail's shaking,
And a grey mist on the sea's face and a grey dawn breaking.

I must down to the seas again, for the call of the running tide
Is a wild call and a clear call that may not be denied;
And all I ask is a windy day with the white clouds flying,
And the flung spray and the blown spume, and the sea-gulls crying.

I must down to the seas again to the vagrant gypsy life.
To the gull's way and the whale's way where the wind's like a whetted knife;
And all I ask is a merry yarn from a laughing fellow-rover,
And the quiet sleep and a sweet dream when the long trick's over.

—John Masefield

Name: _____ Date: _____

Assessment Questions: "Sea Fever"

1. Read the line from the poem and answer the question.

   > *And the flung spray and the blown <u>spume</u>, and the sea-gulls crying.*

   Which word is the **best** synonym for *spume* as it is used in the line?
   - ○ A. foam
   - ○ B. sand
   - ○ C. water
   - ○ D. wave

2. Personification is giving human-like characteristics to an animal, non-living object, or an idea. Which line from the poem uses personification?
   - ○ A. *And all I ask is a tall ship and star to steer her by;*
   - ○ B. *And a grey mist on the sea's face and a grey dawn breaking.*
   - ○ C. *And all I ask is a windy day with the white clouds flying,*
   - ○ D. *And the quiet sleep and a sweet dream when the long trick's over.*

3. Which phrase from the poem is an example of imagery?
   - ○ A. wind's song
   - ○ B. grey mist
   - ○ C. clear call
   - ○ D. gull's way

4. Read the dictionary entry and answer the question.

   > **trick** \'trik\ n 1. an action that is designed to amuse 2. an act of deception 3. taking a trip for your job 4. taking a shift of duty at the wheel of a ship

   Which is the **best** definition for the word *trick* as it is used in stanza 3?
   - ○ A. definition 1
   - ○ B. definition 2
   - ○ C. definition 3
   - ○ D. definition 4

5. Explain how the poet's use of imagery contributes to the meaning of the poem. Support your answer with textual evidence from the poem.

   Write your answer in the box.

Poet: Alfred, Lord Tennyson (1809–1892)
Birthplace: England
Interesting Fact: Tennyson is one of the most popular British poets.

The Throstle

"Summer is coming, summer is coming.
    I know it, I know it, I know it.
Light again, leaf again, life again, love again."
    Yes, my wild little Poet.

Sing the new year in under the blue.
    Last year you sang it as gladly.
"New, new, new, new!" Is it then so new
    That you should carol so madly?

"Love again, song again, nest again, young again,"
    Never a prophet so crazy!
And hardly a daisy as yet, little friend,
    See, there is hardly a daisy.

"Here again, here, here, here, happy year!"
    Oh, warble unchidden, unbidden!
Summer is coming, is coming, my dear,
    And all the winters are hidden.

—Alfred, Lord Tennyson

throstle – bird commonly known as the song thrush

Name: _____ Date: _____

Assessment Questions: "The Throstle"

1. How does the speaker feel about the throstle's caroling?
   - ○ A. He is amused by the throstle's excited caroling.
   - ○ B. He is annoyed by the tedious caroling of the throstle.
   - ○ C. He is charmed by the melodious caroling of the throstle.
   - ○ D. He is irritated by the continuous caroling of the throstle.

2. Which word **best** describes the overall mood of the poem?
   - ○ A. calm
   - ○ B. cheerful
   - ○ C. content
   - ○ D. critical

3. Read the lines from the poem and answer the question.

   > "Summer is coming, summer is coming,
   > I know it, I know it, I know it.

   What is **most likely** the significance of the poet's use of repetition?
   - ○ A. to create a visual image
   - ○ B. to demonstrate the speaker's interest in bird watching
   - ○ C. to describe the bird's ability to forecast the weather
   - ○ D. to reveal the tone of the poem

4. Why does the poet use quotation marks in the poem?
   - ○ A. to emphasize the end of winter and the coming of summer
   - ○ B. to highlight the speaker's feelings about the throstle
   - ○ C. to separate the throstle's voice from the speaker's thoughts
   - ○ D. to stress the importance of the speaker's role

5. Explain how the cycle of seasons is revealed in the poem. Support your answer using textual evidence from the poem.

   Write your answer in the box.

Poet: Henry Wadsworth Longfellow (1807–1882)
Birthplace: Maine
Interesting Fact: One of Longfellow's most famous poems is "Paul Revere's Ride."

The Tide Rises, the Tide Falls

The tide rises, the tide falls,
The twilight darkens, the curlew calls;
Along the sea-sands damp and brown
The traveller hastens toward the town,
    And the tide rises, the tide falls.

Darkness settles on roofs and walls,
But the sea, the sea in the darkness calls;
The little waves, with their soft, white hands,
Efface the footprints in the sands,
    And the tide rises, the tide falls.

The morning breaks; the steeds in their stalls
Stamp and neigh, as the hostler calls;
The day returns, but nevermore
Returns the traveller to the shore,
    And the tide rises, the tide falls.

—Henry Wadsworth Longfellow

Assessment Questions: "The Tide Rises, the Tide Falls"

1. What does the word *darkness* in the poem **most likely** symbolize?
   - ○ A. death
   - ○ B. sadness
   - ○ C. sorrow
   - ○ D. trouble

2. Read the lines from stanza 2 of the poem and answer the question.

   > *The little waves, with their soft, white hands,*
   > *Efface the footprints in the sands,*

   Which is the **best** meaning for the word *efface* as it is used in the stanza?
   - ○ A. to build up
   - ○ B. to smooth away
   - ○ C. to tear down
   - ○ D. to wear down

3. Explain how the passage of time is revealed through the poem. Support your answer with textual evidence from the poem.

   Write your answer in the box.

4. Explain how the author's use of repetition impacts the rhythm of the poem. Support your answer with textual evidence from the poem.

   Write your answer in the box.

Paired Poems

Directions: Read **Poem One** and answer the questions.

Poem One: "A Poison Tree" by William Blake

A Poison Tree

I was angry with my friend:
I told my wrath, my wrath did end.
I was angry with my foe:
I told it not, my wrath did grow.

And I watered it in fears
Night and morning with my tears,
And I sunned it with smiles
And with soft deceitful wiles.

And it grew both day and night,
Till it bore an apple bright,
And my foe beheld it shine,
And he knew that it was mine,—

And into my garden stole
When the night had veiled the pole;
In the morning, glad, I see
My foe outstretched beneath the tree.

—William Blake

wrath – anger
foe – enemy
wiles – tricks
veiled – covered, concealed

Paired Poems (cont.)

Assessment Questions

Use **Poem One**, "A Poison Tree," to answer questions 1–5.

1. Which word **best** describes the theme of the poem?
   - ○ A. anger
   - ○ B. deceit
   - ○ C. hate
   - ○ D. regret

2. Why did the poet **most likely** write the poem?
   - ○ A. to emphasize the importance of forgiveness
   - ○ B. to express his feelings about friendship
   - ○ C. to describe the shame that accompanies deceitful actions
   - ○ D. to reveal the destructive consequences of hate

3. What does the apple symbolize?
   - ○ A. the speaker's feelings of regret
   - ○ B. the hatred the speaker has toward his foe
   - ○ C. the fruit of the speaker's anger
   - ○ D. the speaker's deceitful actions

4. What feelings does the speaker express in the last stanza of the poem?
   - ○ A. annoyance, because his foe had secretly entered the garden
   - ○ B. gladness, because his foe was defeated
   - ○ C. loss, because his foe was no longer around to torment
   - ○ D. regret, because his feelings had caused the death of his foe

5. Explain how the title contributes to the theme of the poem.

   Write your answer in the box.

Paired Poems (cont.)

Directions: Read **Poem Two** and answer the questions.

Poem Two: "Blight" by Edna St. Vincent Millay

Blight

Hard seeds of hate I planted
    That should by now be grown,—
Rough stalks, and from thick stamens
    A poisonous pollen blown,
And odors rank, unbreathable,
    From dark corollas thrown!

At dawn from my damp garden
    I shook the chilly dew;
The thin boughs locked behind me
    That sprang to let me through;
The blossoms slept,—I sought a place
    Where nothing lovely grew.

And there, when day was breaking,
    I knelt and looked around:
The light was near, the silence
    Was palpitant with sound;
I drew my hate from out my breast
    And thrust it in the ground.

Oh, ye so fiercely tended,
    Ye little seeds of hate!
I bent above your growing
    Early and noon and late,
Yet are ye drooped and pitiful,—
    I cannot rear ye straight!

The sun seeks out my garden,
    No nook is left in shade,
No mist nor mold nor mildew
    Endures on any blade,
Sweet rain slants under every bough:
    Ye falter, and ye fade.

—Edna St. Vincent Millay

blight – plant disease caused by fungi
rank – foul; putrid
palpitant – rapidly pulsing

Paired Poems (cont.)

Assessment Questions

Use **Poem Two** "Blight" to answer questions 6–10.

6. **Part A**
   Which word **best** describes the theme of the poem?
   ○ A. apathy
   ○ B. hate
   ○ C. peace
   ○ D. remorse

   Part B
   Which line from the poem is the **most** helpful in understanding the theme?
   ○ A. *Hard seeds of hate I planted*
   ○ B. *Where nothing lovely grew.*
   ○ C. *The light was near, the silence*
   ○ D. *Sweet rain slants under every bough:*

7. What is the meaning of the word *corollas* as it is used in stanza 1?
   ○ A. leaves
   ○ B. petals
   ○ C. roots
   ○ D. stems

8. Personification is giving human-like characteristics to an animal, non-living object, or an idea. Which line from the poem is an example of personification?
   ○ A. *A poisonous pollen blown,*
   ○ B. *The blossoms slept,—I sought a place*
   ○ C. *Was palpitant with sound;*
   ○ D. *No nook is left in shade,*

9. Which line from the poem is an example of the poet's use of imagery?
   ○ A. *And odors rank, unbreathable,*
   ○ B. *That sprang to let me through;*
   ○ C. *Oh, ye so fiercely tended,*
   ○ D. *Ye falter, and ye fade.*

10. Alliteration is the repetition of a consonant sound at the beginning of a series of words. Which line from the poem contains alliteration?
    ○ A. *I shook the chilly dew;*
    ○ B. *I knelt and looked around:*
    ○ C. *Ye little seeds of hate!*
    ○ D. *No mist nor mold nor mildew*

Name: _____ Date: _____

Paired Poems (cont.)

Assessment Questions

Use **Poem One** and **Poem Two** to answer question 11.

11. What do the last stanzas of "A Poison Tree" and "Blight" **most likely** suggest about the speakers in each poem? Use textual evidence from each poem to support your answer.

Write your answer in the box.

Media Integration

The Road Not Taken

Two roads diverged in a yellow wood,
And sorry I could not travel both
And be one traveler, long I stood
And looked down one as far as I could
To where it bent in the undergrowth;

Then took the other, as just as fair,
And having perhaps the better claim,
Because it was grassy and wanted wear;
Though as for that the passing there
Had worn them really about the same,

And both that morning equally lay
In leaves no step had trodden black.
Oh, I kept the first for another day!
Yet knowing how way leads on to way,
I doubted if I should ever come back.

I shall be telling this with a sigh
Somewhere ages and ages hence:
Two roads diverged in a wood, and I—
I took the one less traveled by,
And that has made all the difference.

—Robert Frost

Name: _____ Date: _____

Media Integration (cont.)

Website: <https://www.youtube.com/watch?v=ZzUm0wqhE7E>
"The Road Not Taken" by Robert Frost (read by Alan Bates)

Directions: Read the poem "The Road Not Taken" by Robert Frost. Then go to the website listed above. Watch and listen closely to the reading of the poem "The Road Not Taken." Observe the speaker's delivery of the poem, and record your observations on the chart. Then follow the directions.

Items to Observe	What I Observed...
Facial Expressions	
Tone of Voice	
Pace of Voice	
Volume of Voice	
Effective Use of Pause	

Explain how your observations of the recorded performance affected your understanding of the poem.

Answer Keys

Skill Builders

Alliteration (p. 7)

Poe uses alliteration to create the tone of the poem, which is grief. This is supported by the use of alliteration such as "weak and weary" and "nodded, nearly napping" in stanza 1, which tells us of his physical state. In stanza 2, he addresses his mental state when he says he turned to his books to bring a "surcease of sorrow" for his "lost Lenore."

Allusion (p. 8)

(Answer will include 2 of the 3 lines)

A Pagan, suckled in a creed out worn,

Have sight of Proteus, rising from the sea,

Or hear old Triton blow his wreathed horn.

Hyperbole (p. 9)

1. Hyperbole: *And fired the shot heard round the world;*
   Explanation: A shot cannot be heard all the way around the world.
2. (Answers will vary.)

Imagery (p. 10)

fog trails (sight); mist creeps (sight); whistle of a boat (sound); cries unendingly (sound);

Metaphor (p.11)

She a window flower—Like a window flower the woman was content to stay in a warm place and thrive. She ignored the male who tried to entice her to leave her home and go with him.

And he a winter breeze—Like a winter breeze the male was cold and harsh and quickly departed for somewhere else when his advances were rejected.

Onomatopoeia (p. 12) Words that should be highlighted: *tinkle, tintinnabulation, jingling, tinkling*

Graphic organizers: (Answers will require teacher verification.)

Personification (p. 13)

(Answers will require teacher verification.)

Rhyme/Repetition (p. 14)

Rhyme Scheme: Stanzas 1–5 is ABA; Stanza 6 is ABAA

The repetition of the line "They are all gone away" emphasizes that no one lives in the house any longer because the house has fallen into "ruin and decay." "There is nothing more to say" is repeated to emphasize that it has been so long ago that no one is still alive "To speak them good or ill."

Rhythm (p. 15)

The repetition of the two-syllable word *gallop* creates a mental image in the mind of the reader of a horse galloping. As the reader reads the poem, he mimics the rhythm of a galloping horse.

Simile (p. 16)

Simile: *"O my Luve's like a red, red rose, That's newly sprung in June:"*

Things Being Compared: Luve (love) and a rose

How are they alike? Luve and the red rose sprung in June have just begun to blossom.

Simile: *"O my Luve's like the melodie, That's sweetly play'd in tune."*

Things Being Compared: Luve and a melodie played in tune

How are they alike? Like a melodie that is played in tune, his love is harmonious and perfect.

Structure (p. 17)

1. two 2. four 3. "Who has seen the wind?"
4. The last three lines of stanza 1 or 2 should be circled.

Symbolism (p. 18)

(Answers will vary but may include.)

1. Answer has been done for you. 2. elderly; weak and weary 3. desolation; loneliness
4. unobtainable; inaccessible 5. speed; quickness

Theme (p. 19)

The overall theme of the poem is hope. While the speaker seems to be sad and mournful at the time, he realizes that even though his life may be "dark and dreary" like the weather, he can still have hope that his condition is temporary because "Behind the clouds is the sun still shining."

Tone and Mood (p. 20)

(Answers may vary, but may include)

Tone: friendly

Words to help identify: You come too;

Connotation: positive

Mood: peaceful or nostalgic

Words to help identify: pasture spring; rake the leaves; little calf; mother

Connotation: positive

Word Meaning (p. 21)

(Answers will require teacher verification.)

Assessment Prep

Count That Day Lost (p. 23)

    1. B   2. D   3. A   4. A

    5. (Answers will vary but should include) The last stanza contributes to the theme because it reveals the consequence of not performing an act of kindness or good deed every day. The consequence for inaction makes the day "worse than lost." In other words, one day of that person's life has been wasted.

Don't Give Up (p. 25)

    1. B   2. B   3. C   4. Part A: C; Part B: A

    5. (Answers will vary but should include) The last stanza of the poem means hard work and perseverance builds character and gains the respect of others.

Escape at Bedtime (p. 27)

    1. A   2. C   3. Part A: C; Part B: A   4. D, E 5. D

The Flag Goes By (p. 29)

    1. Part A: B; Part B: D   2. C   3. D   4. A   5. C

The Flight of Youth (p. 31)

    1. A   2. C   3. Part A: A; Part B: B   4. B, D 5. B

The Glory of the Day Was in Her Face (p. 33)

    1. C   2. B   3. D   4. A

    5. (Answers will vary but should include) In the first two stanzas, the tone of the poem is passionate. The speaker is zealous in his adoration of the female's face, voice, and smile, comparing them to the night, the morning, and melodious music. In stanza 3, the speaker compares his numbness of feelings to someone who is dead because she is no longer with him.

Hope (p. 35)

    1. C   2. D   3. B

    4. (Answers will vary but may include) In the first four stanzas, Hope was too fearful and "timid" to take action, but while she was still present the tone remains hopeful. In the last stanza, hope leaves, and therefore the tone changes from hopeful to hopeless.

I Wandered Lonely as a Cloud (p. 37)

    1. C   2. A   3. D

    4. (Answers will vary but should include) In stanza 4, the speaker says that often when he is at home, lying on his couch in a "pensive mood," the memory of the daffodils will "flash upon" his "inward eye." He describes this as the "bliss of solitude." The joy of the memory gives him pleasure and his heart "dances with the daffodils." In stanza 3, the speaker states that while he "gazed—and gazed" on the daffodils, he didn't think anything about the "wealth the show to me

had brought." The reader now understands that the insignificant event did become an important event, because the "wealth" mentioned in stanza 3 is the joy the speaker receives from recalling the memory of the daffodils.

Love and Friendship (p. 39)
1. C   2. D   3. D
4. (Answers will vary but should include) In the poem "Love and Friendship," the poet uses a simile to compare love to a wild rose-briar. The poet most likely did this because a rose is often used to symbolize love and passion. However, the rose also has a thorny stem that can symbolize the difficulties in a relationship. The poet uses the attributes of a rose to describe love. The poet reminds the reader that "The wild rose-briar is "sweet in spring" and "Its summer blossoms scent the air." Both of these lines mention seasons. This lets the reader know that for a season love can be wonderful. In the line "That, when December blights thy brow," the poet reminds the reader that as a rose can be blighted by a disease causing its death, so can difficulties lead to the death of love.
5. (Answers will vary but should include) In stanzas 1 and 2, the poet is making a comparison between love and friendship. She questions, "which will bloom most constantly?" Stanza 3 is important, because she shares her conclusion with the reader. She decides to "scorn" love and "deck" herself with friendship, because friendship will remain when difficulties arise, while love may not survive "when December blights thy brow."

Meeting at Night (p. 41)
1. Part A: B; Part B: D   2. C   3. D   4. A
5. (Answers will vary but may include) In stanza 1, the speaker is describing sights he sees while sailing at nighttime such as "The gray sea and the long black land; And the yellow half-moon large and low." This leads the reader to think the theme of the poem is sailing. In the last four lines of stanza 2, the reader discovers that sailing is not of primary importance but only a step he takes for his true purpose of secretly meeting with his love.

The Railway Train (p. 43)
1. C   2. B
3. (Answers will vary but may include) In stanza 1 the poet starts out by saying "I like to see" the train. However, when she begins describing the train, she describes it using words and phrases with negative connotations such as *prodigious, supercilious peer, complaining,* and *horrid hooting.* This leads the reader to think that while she is fascinated by watching the train, she really doesn't like it.
4. (Answers will vary but should include) The words *lick, step, peer, crawl, complaining, chase,* and *docile,* are human-like characteristics used to describe the train. These examples of personification help the reader to visualize the train's movement.

The Sandpiper (p. 45)
1. B   2. A   3. B   4. B
5. (Answers will vary but may include) Line one of the poem reveals that the sandpiper and the speaker are alone on the beach. The poet repeatedly uses the phrase "the little sandpiper and I" in each stanza to emphasize the fact they remain alone on the beach.

Sea Fever (p. 47)
1. A   2. B   3. B   4. D
5. (Answers will vary but should include) In the poem, the speaker expresses his strong desire to return to the sea. Images such as "a tall ship," "white sail's shaking," "grey dawn breaking," "white clouds flying," and "sea-gulls crying" appeal to the reader's physical senses and help to create a vivid mental picture of what the speaker misses most about traveling on the sea.

The Throstle (p. 49)
1. A   2. B   3. D   4. C
5. (Answers will vary but should include) The poet reveals the cycle of the seasons through the words of the speaker and his interpretation of the throstle's caroling. This is evidenced in the lines "Sing the new year in under the blue. / Last year you sang it as gladly." and "Summer is coming, is coming, my dear, / And all the winters are hidden."

The Tide Rises, the Tide Falls (p. 51)
1. A   2. B
3. (Answers will vary but should include) The first line in stanza 1 talks about the rising and falling of the tide. This phrase is repeated in all 3 stanzas. The poet is reminding the reader that this cycle is a never-ending, daily event. Another daily event is the cycle of day and night. In stanza 1, the phrase "the twilight darkens" refers to the approaching of night. In stanza 2, the darkness has settled "on roofs and walls" meaning nighttime has arrived. The first line in stanza 3 contains the phrase "the morning breaks." This shows the cycle of day and night begins again. Lastly, the symbolic representation of the passage of a person's lifetime can be seen in the phrase "footprints in the sand."
4. (Answers will vary but should include) The first line in stanza 1 states "The tide rises, the tide falls." This phrase is repeated in all 3 stanzas. The poet uses the repetition of this line to create a rhythm which mimics the effect of a tide coming in and going out.

Paired Poems (p. 53–56)
1. C   2. D   3. C   4. B
5. (Answers will vary but may include) The title of the poem is "A Poison Tree." Poison is a substance that is usually used to kill something. Tree refers to something that is alive, growing, and if it is nurtured, something that will bear fruit. The title contributes to the poem's theme of hate because hate is a feeling that will "poison" your thoughts and feelings. If nurtured, it will bear fruit that may result in destructive actions.
6. Part A: B; Part B: A   7. B   8. B   9. A   10. D
11. (Answers will vary but should include) In the last stanza of the poem "A Poison Tree," the speaker states he is glad his foe is dead. This shows the speaker is a person who does not feel remorse for his destructive thoughts and actions. In the last stanza of the poem "Blight," the words *my garden* symbolizes the speaker's feelings. The words *mold* and *mildew* indicate a blight has struck her garden. In other words, blight symbolizes her feelings of hate. The speaker reveals she no longer has feelings of hate because "No mist nor mold nor mildew / Endures on any blade." This shows the speaker is a person who can forgive and forget.

Media Integration (p.58)
Chart: (Answers will require teacher verification.)
Constructed Response: (Answers will require teacher verification.)